FEAR : THE ENEMY OF CHANGE

DEFEATING FALSE EVIDENCE APPEARING REAL IN LIFE

James BLESSINGS

TABLE OF CONTENT

CHAPTER 1

WHAT IS FEAR

Fear is a strongly horrendous feeling in light of seeing or perceiving a risk or danger. Dread causes physiological changes that might create conduct responses like mounting a forceful reaction or escaping the danger. Dread in people might happen because of a specific upgrade happening in the present, or expectation or assumption for a future danger seen as a gamble to oneself. The trepidation reaction emerges from the view of risk prompting a showdown with or escape from/keeping away from the danger (otherwise called the survival reaction), which is outrageous instances of dread (frightfulness and fear) can be a freeze reaction or loss of motion.

A young lady giving indications of dread and nervousness in a dubious climate
In people and different creatures, dread is balanced by the course of cognizance and learning. Accordingly, dread is decided as judicious or proper and nonsensical or improper. A silly trepidation is known as fear.

Dread is firmly connected with the feeling of nervousness, which happens as the consequence of dangers that are seen to be wild or inescapable. The trepidation reaction serves endurance by inciting fitting conduct reactions, so it has been saved all through development. The humanistic and authoritative examination additionally proposes that people's apprehensions are not exclusively subject to their inclination but rather are likewise molded by their social relations and culture, which guide how they might interpret when and how much trepidation to feel.[3][page needed]

Dread is now and again erroneously viewed as something contrary to boldness. Since fortitude is a readiness to confront difficulty, dread is an illustration of a condition that makes the activity of boldness conceivable.

Numerous physiological changes in the body are related to dread, summed up as the survival reaction. A natural reaction for adapting to risk, it works by speeding up the breathing rate (hyperventilation), pulse, vasoconstriction of the fringe veins prompting blood pooling, expanding muscle strain including the muscles connected to every hair follicle to the agreement, and causing "goosebumps", or all the more clinically, piloerection (making a chilly individual hotter or a scared creature look more noteworthy), perspiring, expanded blood glucose (hyperglycemia), expanded serum calcium, expansion in white platelets called neutrophilic leukocytes, sharpness prompting rest aggravation and "butterflies in the stomach" (dyspepsia). This crude component might assist a life form with making due by either taking off or battling the risk. With the series of physiological changes, the awareness understands a feeling of dread.

CHAPTER 2

Confidence VRS FEAR

Confidence and dread can't exist together. Confidence is portrayed in Hebrews 11:1 as being "sure of what we don't have any idea." It is an outright conviction that God is continually working in the background in each part of our lives, in any event, when there is no unmistakable proof to help that reality. Then again, dread, just expressed, is unbelief or powerless conviction. As unbelief acquires the advantage in our viewpoints, dread grabs hold of our feelings. Our liberation from dread and stress depends on trust, which is the exact inverse of unbelief. We want to comprehend that confidence isn't something that we can create in ourselves. Confidence is a gift

(Ephesians 2:8-9), and dedication is portrayed as a natural product (or trademark) that is created in our lives by the Holy Spirit (Galatians 5:22-23). The Christian's confidence is a certain confirmation in a God who loves us, who understands our thought processes, and who thinks often about our most profound requirements. That confidence keeps on developing as we concentrate on the Bible and gain proficiency with the properties of His astonishing person. The more we find out about God, the more we can see Him working in our lives and the more grounded our confidence develops.

Developing confidence is what we want to have and what God wants to create in us. In any case, how, in everyday life, could we at any point foster confidence that vanquishes our feelings of dread? According to the Bible, "Confidence stops by endlessly hearing by the Word of God" (Romans 10:17). The cautious investigation of God's

Word is of essential significance in fostering areas of strength for a. God believes that us should know Him and depend on His bearing in our lives. It's through the meeting, perusing, and contemplation in the Scriptures that we start to encounter serious areas of strength for confidence that rejects stress and dread. Investing energy in the petition and calm love fosters a relationship with our superb Father that sees us through even the haziest of evenings. In the Psalms, we see an image of David, who, similar to us, encountered seasons of dread. Song 56:3 uncovers his confidence with these words: "When I am apprehensive, I will confide in you." Psalm 119 is loaded up with sections communicating how David prized God's Word: "I look for you with my entire being; don't allow me to wander from your orders" (stanza 10); "I reflect on your statutes and think about your methodologies" (refrain 15); "I have stowed away your statement in my heart that I probably won't sin against you" (refrain 11). These are uncovering words that express insight to us today.

God is caring and understanding toward our shortcomings, however, He expects us to proceed in confidence, and the Bible is evident that confidence doesn't develop and fortify without preliminaries. The difficulty is God's best instrument to foster areas of strength for a. That example is clear in Scripture. God takes every single one of us through unfortunate circumstances, and, as we figure out how to comply with God's Word and permit it to immerse our contemplations, we find every preliminary turns into a venturing stone to a more grounded and more profound confidence. It enables us to say, "He supported me before, he'll bring me through today and he'll maintain me later on!" God worked this way in David's life. At the point when David elected to battle against Goliath, he said, "The Lord who conveyed me from the paw of the lion and the paw of the bear will convey me from the hand of this Philistine" (1 Samuel 17:37). David knew the God who had supported him through hazardous circumstances before. He had seen and encountered God's power and security in his life, and this created upon dauntless confidence.

The Word of God is rich with guarantees for us to grab hold of and guarantee for ourselves. At the point when we face monetary difficulty, Philippians 4:19 tells us, "And my God will supply every one of your requirements as per His wealth in greatness in Christ Jesus." If we are restless about a future choice, Psalm 32:8 advises us that God will "train you and show you in the manner in which you ought to go; I will direct you with my eye upon you." In disorder we can recollect that Romans 5:3-5 says, "thus, however we likewise magnificence in our sufferings, since we know that enduring produces diligence; tirelessness, endlessly character, trust.

Furthermore, trust doesn't embarrass us, since God's affection has been emptied into our souls through the Holy Spirit, who has been given to us." If somebody betrays us, we can be helped by the words in Romans 8:31, "Assuming God is for us who can be against us!" Throughout life, we will keep on confronting different preliminaries that would cause us dread, yet God guarantees us that we can know a quiet harmony through each circumstance: "Don't be restless about anything, yet in each circumstance, by supplication and appeal, with thanksgiving, present your solicitations to God. What's more, the tranquility of God, which rises above all comprehension, will monitor your hearts and your brains in Christ Jesus" (Philippians 4:7).

CHAPTER 3

FEARS TO CONQUER FOR A SUCCESSFUL LIFE :

-Anxiety toward WHAT OTHER PEOPLE THINK

If you have any desire to be your best and perform at a significant level, anxiety toward individuals' viewpoints might be keeping you down.

Ponder when you were very restless — say, before facing freely talk, lifting your hand in a major gathering, or any event, strolling through a room of outsiders. The explanation you felt a little frightened and tense is you were stressed over friendly dissatisfaction.

Our apprehension about others' perspectives, or FOPO as I call it, has turned into a nonsensical and useless fixation in the advanced world, and its adverse consequences reach a long way past presentation.

If you begin saving money and less consideration regarding what makes you — your abilities, convictions, and values — and begin adjusting to what others might think, you'll hurt your true capacity. You'll begin avoiding any risks since you're anxious about what will occur on the opposite side of the scrutinize. You'll fear being criticized or dismissed. When tested, you'll give up your perspective. You won't lift your hand when you have no control over the result. You will not go for that advancement since you won't believe you're qualified.

Sadly, FOPO is essential for the human condition since we're working with an old mind. A desire for social endorsement made our predecessors wary and keen; millennia prior, on the off chance that the obligation regarding the bombed chase fell on your shoulders, your spot in the clan could be undermined. The craving to fit in and the deadening apprehension about being hated subvert our capacity to seek after the lives we need to make.

This highlights why we want to prepare and condition our brain — so the smaller part isn't manipulating everything else.

Assuming you end up encountering FOPO, there are ways of hosing the force of your pressure reactions. When you're mindful of your viewpoints, guide yourself toward certainty-building explanations (I am a decent open speaker, I've invested the effort with the goal that I can believe my capacities, I have a ton of extraordinary comments, I'm ready for this advancement). These assertions will assist you with zeroing in on your abilities and capacities as opposed to others' perspectives. Take full breaths, as well. This will indicate to your mind that you're not in impending peril.

However, to vanquish FOPO, you'll have to develop more mindfulness. The greater part of us carry on with an existence with a general feeling of what our identity is, and, in a ton of conditions, no more. We scrape by. Be that as it may, to be your best while being less unfortunate of individuals' viewpoints, you want to foster a more grounded and a lot further feeling of what your identity is.

You can begin by fostering an individual way of thinking – a word or expression that communicates your fundamental convictions and values. The individual way of thinking of Pete Carroll, my colleague and lead trainer of the Seattle Seahawks, is "consistently contend." For Coach Carroll, continuously contending implies going through each day striving to improve and arrive at his fullest potential. This way of thinking isn't a saying or motto; rather, it's his compass, directing his activities, considerations, and choices. As a mentor. A dad. A companion. In each everyday issue.

While concocting an individual way of thinking, pose yourself a progression of inquiries:

When I'm at my best, what convictions lie just underneath the outer layer of my viewpoints and activities?

Who are individuals that exhibit attributes and characteristics that are in arrangement with mine?

What are those characteristics?

What are your number one statements? Your #1 words?

Whenever you've responded to these inquiries, circle the words that stand apart to you and cross out the ones that don't. In the wake of concentrating on what's left side, attempt to think of an expression or sentence that lines up with precisely what your identity is and how you need to carry on with your life. Share the draft with a friend or family member, request information, and tweak your way of thinking from that point. Then, at that point, commit it to memory and return to it day to day.

Creating an individual way of thinking can be an enlightening and strong activity. At the point when I mentor groups of chiefs, I frequently request that they record their way of thinking and offer it to the gathering. I will always remember the time a senior chief wowed everybody in the room. As tears gushed in his eyes, he fixed his back, held his head high, and said, "My way of thinking is to walk commendable." He let his partners know that his folks were migrants who had endured provoking conditions to guarantee he would be advised to amazing open doors. On account of his folks' diligent effort and penance, he thought of it as his obligation to carry on with life as though his family peak were embellished across his chest. Consistently, he attempts to genuinely deserve their great deeds and to be an incredibly good example for the future.

I can't exaggerate how significant an individual way of thinking is. Working with NFL players and mentors, outrageous game competitors, and senior pioneers at Fortune 50 organizations, that's what I've seen, past a steady quest for being their best, what makes these superior workers extraordinary is their reasonable feeling of the rules that guide them. Due to their clearness, they're more ready to propel themselves, find out more, and embrace uneasiness. They can close out the commotion and assessments of fans and media and pay attention to their own all-around aligned, sense of direction.

Whenever you've fostered your very own way of thinking, subscribe to live as per its principles. Begin at home. Tell that individual you love them. Dance at a wedding. Face challenges. Be deferentially odd. (That presumably implies, be you.) Then attempt it at work. Give a show. Go for that advancement. Do things that will incite the assessments of others. At the point when you feel the force of FOPO keeping you down, essentially recognize it, and once again associate it with your way of thinking and the bigger target within reach.

Pushing ahead, request input from a short rundown of individuals who make a difference to you. Genuine reflection is a crucial part of dominance. During an episode of my webcast, "Tracking down Mastery," Brené Brown, a famous specialist and creator of Dare to Lead, proposed that the names of those individuals ought to fit on a 1×1 inch record card. I add a subsequent condition. Individuals on your card ought to have an incredible feeling of the individual you are and the individual you're attempting to turn into. Respect their perspectives, letting the clamor from the group disappear. Adjust their criticism with your experience.

In particular, recollect that development and learning occur while you're working at the edge of your ability. Like exploding an almost swelled expansion, living as per your way of thinking will require more exertion and power, be that as it may, the outcome, which is to truly and creatively express what your identity is, will push you to live and work with more reason and significance. The feeling of dread toward change

-THE FEAR OF MAKING THE WRONG DECISION

In both school and throughout everyday life, you are normally going to be confronted with a ton of choices. A few decisions will feel like they are a higher priority than others. The scope of choices you make consistently influences your life in various ways, a large portion of which are obscure to you at the hour of the direction. Certain individuals are so stressed over settling on off-base choices that they experience the ill effects of decidophobia or anxiety about deciding.

There's a distinction between finding an opportunity to gauge your choices and being so ridden with nervousness that you stay away from the interaction out and out. We will separate the meaning of decidophobia, the side effects of decidophobia, and afterward, offer tips to assist you with defeating this trepidation. Regardless of whether you experience the ill effects of this condition, everybody can profit from the accommodating dynamic counsel in this article.

Thinking man with a hands-on mouth Photograph by Nathan Dumlao on Unsplash

What is Decidophobia?

Decidophobia is characterized as the "nonsensical anxiety toward simply deciding." In its most outrageous structure, the people who have this dread might encounter all outfits of anxiety while pondering and settling on a choice. Fits of anxiety cause your pulse and breathing to accelerate, circulatory strain to rise, perspiring, muscle pressure, and shudder.

To keep away from these sentiments, individuals with decidophobia may try not to be put in circumstances where they should settle on a choice. Be that as it may, this could become problematic, particularly if you are an understudy who requires you to conclude things like your major, your school of decision, and your timetable, and that's just the beginning.

Before we share how to defeat decidophobia, here's a rundown of normal side effects related to this trepidation.

Side effects of Decidophobia:
Tension
Fits of anxiety
Muscle strain and extreme perspiring
Expanded reliance on others for direction
You believe you're mystic
Powerlessness to adapt to the tension around deciding

What Causes the Fear of Making Decisions?
If you are somebody who feels like they have piety about deciding, you're presumably asking why you have this fear. While there is no careful reason, specialists have conjectured that it might have originated from a horrendous mishap.

Furthermore, on the off chance that one experiences a horrible mishap that is genuinely excruciating and has a hereditary inclination to fostering psychological instability, it could intensify what is going on.

Choices might be confounding or startling to adapt to given a difficult occasion during youth. This is particularly evident on the off chance that the choice within reach causes you to feel feeble or like you might need control.

Also, choices might appear to be more excellent if:

1. Life partners will be impacted by the decision

2. Cash assumes a part

3. There's a feeling of dread toward passing up a great opportunity (FOMO)

4. You need trust in the circumstance

5. The choice will include more work

6. There's companion pressure

The Side Effects of Fear of Making Decisions
Dreading settling on a choice will influence your life and connections.

A portion of the unfortunate results related to this fear include:

Passing up connections
Losing a chance for advancement at work
Absence of movement encounters
Cash issues since you can't choose what to put resources into or the amount to save

These results decisively affect one's satisfaction. Accordingly, it's vital to do whatever it takes to defeat decidophobia.

Yoga and care reflection to diminish tension

Tips to Help You Cope with Decidophobia
If you are experiencing decidophobia, or know somebody who does, here are a few techniques to attempt to defeat the anxiety

toward deciding, or the anxiety toward accomplishing something wrong:

1. Take Actionable Decisions:

It's OK to recognize that settling on a choice is unnerving. However, to "break the chains," you simply need to let it all out and overcome the trepidation by pursuing a decision.
Attempt The Decision-Making Quadrant: Use a network (chart) like the one underneath to classify your choices by: dire/not critical and significant/not significant.

2. Lessen the Number Of Decisions:

One of the most incredible ways of beating the anxiety toward pursuing choices is to get yourself positioned to make less of them consistently. For instance, you can do this by making a dinner plan and adhering to it or by wearing similar fundamental garments regularly (this is the kind of thing Steve Jobs did so he could think carefully and power on greater choices).

3. Be Curious:

Make little strides towards picking. You can do this by posing yourself the accompanying inquiries, "What's the most terrible result that is conceivable?" "What is the probability this will happen?" "Imagine a scenario where the work helps me out."

4. Shift Your Point of View:

Attempt to envision confronting the decision as another person other than yourself. You can do this by asking yourself, "How might X respond?" Then, you can attempt to step beyond yourself to see what is going on within reach and assess your subsequent stage.

5. Enable Yourself:

After asking yourself the best-and most pessimistic scenario results, consider that the most pessimistic scenario result might occur. However, at that point advise yourself that you can and you will defeat it. Truth be told, the chance of an adverse result can likewise offer a chance for development. By moving your mentality towards energy, you can prepare yourself to deal with any test.

6. Know Your Why:

By putting forth your three principal objectives, or needs, you can continuously begin with the choices that assist to accomplish these. Accordingly, you will want to go after the choices that are more significant first. Assuming that you ask yourself, "Will this assist me with accomplishing that?" and the response is "no" or "not as of now," let that choice stand by and address a need all things considered.

7. See Both Sides of Risk:

As a rule, when a decision appears to be dangerous or terrifying, this is because the unfortunate result is extremely important to you. Yet, make certain to think about the contrary side of the coin, as in what will occur if you don't make the move? This could be similar or more regrettable than going with a decision that appears to be frightening in any case.

8. Gain from Mistakes:

Thus, you committed an error once, two times, or on different occasions that felt "wrong." You realized this since you made the move and needed to manage a not exactly ideal result. Be that as it may, consider this as an example since now you are more educated for the following time you settle on a comparable choice. This will just occur with training, missteps, and gaining from everything.

9. Inhale and Breathing Therapy:

At the point when you have fits of anxiety or tension, the main counteractant is to have the option to recapture control of your relaxation. You ought to work on returning to your breath by zeroing in on the manner your chest and mid-region rise and fall with your breath in and breathe out. You can count your breaths and match you you're feathered n your bin with your breath tool.

10. Mental Behavioral Therapy:

For certain individuals, looking for proficient assistance is an effective method for defeating decidophobia. A specialist might manage mental conduct treatment (CBT) with you to reveal the hidden motivations behind why you experience the ill effects of decidophobia. Then they will offer strategies to defeat these sentiments.

11. Request Help:

You ought to constantly recollect that you have support when you decide. Whether you select to ask a companion, a relative, a scholarly counsel, a guide, a chief, or another person in your circle, some individuals need to see you succeed. Accordingly, they will offer help in your period of scarcity.

12. Pay attention to Your Gut:

In many occurrences, your stomach has the right response before you even have the opportunity to contemplate decisions. You ought to pay attention to your stomach and trust it because these hunches come from sense.

13. Stress Less Over Failing:

Attempt to advise yourself that the result isn't the main important thing. On the off chance that you fall flat, you can attempt once more. Most decisions aren't super durable in any case and there are ways of rectifying botches.

14. Practice Yoga and Mindfulness:

One more method for beating general nervousness and alleviating pressure is to exercise or practice yoga and care. Yoga is both a psychological and actual activity that can assist you with zeroing in on being available, similar to care. At the point when you are available, you are more ready to see plainly and center around what's before you in the present time and place. This can assist you with reducing your uneasiness and feeling of dread toward the future or disappointment.

Significant Reminders

The fact that fear is an inclination makes it critical's helpful. An inclination originates from apparent danger. On the off chance that you can prepare your psyche to acknowledge how you feel, acknowledge that there's by and large not a reasonable "wrong" or "right" approach, and that your instinct might try and depend on a dread for development, then, at that point, you can turn out to be more content with the dynamic cycle.

Another strategy is to go for the gold you can, as opposed to going for the ideal result. Utilizing a procedure of "satisficing," or going for the gold, can permit you to pick arrangements and keep away from overthinking or encountering lament.

The Different Levels of Decision-Makers
Despite choices, your body normally enters a condition of battle, flight, or freeze.

Here are the various degrees of dynamic you might insight as you work your direction towards turning into a Level 5 chief!

Level 1 - Freeze

Now and again, the apprehension about direction is overpowering to such an extent that it causes a loss of motion. This level is the point at which somebody feels so frightened and numb that they will keep away from the choice completely.

Level 2 - Passive Pleasing

The individual who decides rather satisfy others instead of themselves assimilates their sentiments. This might be alright outwardly, but in any case, they are building sensations of outrage and hatred inside. Thusly, it's inevitable before they will detonate.

Level 3 - Sitting in the Middle

Certain individuals might depend on remaining in decisions. For instance, assuming that somebody is requesting that

they decide to cast a ballot liberal or moderate, they may simply swim in the center.
For the present moment, this could work. Yet, with regards to workplace issues or life choices, a more self-assured individual will dominate and compel their course in for sure except if the individual in the center chooses to make some noise.

Level 4 - Assertive Action

At the point when you know your convictions and where you stand, you can express your real thoughts. Albeit shouting out may influence others now and again, it for the most part leads in the correct bearing since great decisions breed great results. These are individuals who start to lead the pack and settle on choices for the people who like to sit back.

Level 5 - Energetic and Enthusiastic

At the point when somebody arrives at this level, they make certain of what they need and what their identity is. They feel engaged, pursue choices that line up with their motivation, and could in fact be persuasive to people around them to partake in dynamic and energetic navigation.

-THE FEAR OF MISSING OUT ON SOMETHING BETTER

Anxiety toward passing up a major opportunity (FOMO) is the sensation of trepidation that one is either not in the loop or passing up data, occasions, encounters, or life choices that could improve one's life.

FOMO is likewise connected with apprehension about lament, which might prompt worries that one could pass up on a chance for social cooperation, a clever encounter, a vital occasion, or productive speculation. It is portrayed by a longing to remain constantly associated with what others are doing and can be depicted as the trepidation that choosing not to partake in some unacceptable decision. FOMO could result from not being familiar with a discussion, missing a TV show, not going to a wedding or party, or hearing that others have found another café. FOMO as of late has been credited with various negative mental and social side effects.

Cell phones empower individuals to constantly keep in touch with their social and expert organizations. This might bring about habitual checking for notices and messages, inspired by a paranoid fear of passing up on an open door.

FOMO has expanded as of late because of progressions in innovation. Long-range informal communication locales set out many open doors for FOMO. While it gives potential open doors to social commitment, it offers a view into a perpetual stream of exercises in which an individual isn't involved. Mental reliance on online entertainment can prompt FOMO or even obsessive web use. FOMO is likewise present in computer games, money management, and business promotion. The rising ubiquity of the expression has prompted related etymological and social variants.FOMO is related to deteriorating despondency and tension and getting down personal satisfaction.

FOMO can likewise influence organizations. Publicity and patterns can lead business pioneers to contribute give givens of what others are doing, as opposed to their business procedure.

The term FOMO (feeling of dread toward passing up a major opportunity) could have been begotten in the period of virtual entertainment, yet it's anything but another idea. Notwithstanding age, we've most likely completely had an encounter where we've felt the terrible sting of FOMO. You can't come to a show with your companions and go the entire evening considering where you're going wrong. Some colleagues go to another spot down the road for lunch while you question whether they're holding without you. It's enticing to summarize it by saying "the grass is generally greener" — yet FOMO is more profound than that. There's a logical premise to this mental response.

Alright, so what's the brain research behind FOMO?
FROM

Research recommends that individuals are two times as impacted by misfortunes as they are by gains. So it's a good idea that our impulse is to stay away from the aggravation of passing up a major opportunity, and harp on our loss on the off chance that we do. Two experts in social financial matters, Daniel Kahneman and Amos Tversky spearheaded the possibility of misfortune repugnance, which sums up how individuals need to stay away from misfortune no matter what.

Good, so that is important for it — we're wired to abstain from missing out on things, including encounters. In any case, there's one more side of the coin to take a gander at as well.

Clinician Barry Schwartz would likewise add that we have such a large number of decisions. We generally consider having choices something to be thankful for, yet there comes where there are simply an excessive number of things to browse! Schwartz depicts this thought exhaustively with his book (and TED Talk) "The Paradox of Choice: Why More Is Less": "Figuring out how to pick is hard. Figuring out how to pick well is more earnestly. Furthermore, figuring out how to pick well in a universe of limitless conceivable outcomes is more earnestly still, maybe excessively hard."

What sets off this apprehension about passing up a major opportunity?
FROM

We should clear up something without skipping a beat: Although virtual entertainment might give us more noteworthy admittance to FOMO, one investigation discovered that catching wind of a botched open door from a companion delivered a similar measure of FOMO as re-reviewing-reviewing entertainment. So one type of correspondence doesn't beat the other, web-based entertainment is simply more open.

One thing that creates a more noteworthy degree of FOMO is passing up a great opportunity in light of a commitment like working or considering. Be that as it may, hey now, who would prefer to work than go out with companions? On the other side, there was still FOMO present in any event, when the subjects were having fun.

The concentrate likewise tried against various sorts of characters and observed that FOMO is essentially an all-inclusive encounter.

How would we beat FOMO unequivocally?
FROM

With regards to diminishing or in any event, killing the apprehension about passing up a great opportunity, the situation is care. Work on being available at the time and appreciative of what you're encountering. Develop non-judgemental mindfulness while living in the present without doling out any gloomy sentiments to things you have zero control over. Quite difficult, sure. Be that as it may, reflection is an extraordinary method for kicking start this new propensity of yours.

Furthermore, keeping by the possibility that more isn't generally better, attempt to restrict your decisions. One method for doing this is to remove any encounters that won't provide you with a genuine sensation of fulfillment. Truly pause for a minute to inquire, "What will I truly escape this?" before you focus on something.

You can likewise take comfort in the way that FOMO diminishes with age. So assuming you're feeling especially wrecked by missing that party, simply sit back and relax — you'll kind of outgrow it.

-Anxiety toward NOT BEING GOOD ENOUGH

The most effective method to Overcome A Fear Of Not Being Good Enough

Like some other relationship, the one you have with yourself ought to be supported. In any case, over the long run, life can change and negative circumstances can stomp on your certainty. It tends to be difficult to conquer your apprehension about not being adequate when you continually need self-assurance. You could want to surrender and mature in your self-opposed, however, you ought to attempt to make something happen and take full advantage of it. For this reason, finding the wellspring of the problem is significant. For what reason do such countless individuals accept they're not adequate? Is it part of their DNA? Indeed, it very well may be.

"According to a ladies' viewpoint, I think there is most certainly a physiological part. Ladies' cerebrums are wired uniquely in contrast to men. Regardless of the orientation, I solidly accept that there's likewise an ecological part that occasionally originates before adulthood and returns to youth. Assumptions are set in the school or social conditions we experience as kids and commonly, those thoughts carry on through adulthood," says Vice President of HR and authoritative advancement for Paychex Laurie Zaucha in a meeting with Bustle over email.

Be that as it may, regardless of whether these things happen doesn't mean these sentiments will remain with you until the end of time. You have control of your current circumstance and what you choose to encircle yourself with can decide how you will see life. That is the reason it's so essential to be careful about who you spend time with and how you choose to converse with yourself. It tends to be debilitating (and exhausting) to face a daily reality such that you prevent yourself from encountering life since you're reluctant to bomb You should be blissful, and the main way life will change is on the off chance that you roll out certain improvements, as well. Now is the ideal time to get life by the horns and figure out how to conquer your apprehension about not being sufficient.

1. Track down The Root Of The Fear

You really must find the wellspring of why you have this impression. The better you comprehend the explanation, the more straightforward it very well may be to survive. "You want to check out at the base of this trepidation. Is it situated in any reality, or is it situated in what we see others are considering us? Ordinarily, this isn't precise, and in the name of full disclosure, we would be kinder to ourselves and concede that nobody is letting us know we are not adequate however ourselves. Assuming we permit ourselves to have the considerations and convictions that what individuals express decidedly about us may be valid, we begin to sow the seeds of feeling sufficient.

2. Counterfeit It Until You Make It

"If you're not certain, imagine that you are. Certainty can be faked — or maybe a better-made sense of, certainty can be learned, rehearsed, and fabricated. The more you make it happen, the better you'll be," says Zaucha. While you would rather not claim to be somebody else, you need to develop yourself from the inside so you can turn out to be more sure about the long run.

3. Center Around Past Successes

At times it's difficult to be positive when your ongoing circumstance isn't solid. Yet, when that occurs, contemplate your previous victories to assist you with conquering your apprehension about not being sufficient. "Center around past triumphs. Recollect how you overcome a test or accomplish a specific objective. Replay that inclination to you. Envision a fruitful result again and again," says Zaucha.

4. Open Yourself To The Feared Activity

One of the most outstanding approaches to over your apprehension about not being sufficient is by really doing what you dread the most. "Assuming that you dread an action or an occasion or an association with someone else, the most effective way to overcome the apprehension (given examination) is to open yourself to the dreaded movement. Openness (and continuous increment of openness) can assist with mitigating dread and uneasiness around feeling lacking. At any rate, at the point when you dread you will not perform 'alright' or 'impeccably' do it. This, thus, will assist with supporting confidence and character," says authorized clinical analyst Dr. Kim Chronister in a meeting with Bustle over email.

5. Try not to Use Self-Deprecating Language

Now is the ideal time to put stock in the most natural sounding way for you when you impart them to others. You would rather not dismiss your considerations since you don't believe they're sufficient or apprehensive that another person won't care for them. "Have a perspective. Try not to utilize limiting expressions like 'I was simply thinking ... ' or 'I could be off-base, however ... ' Make explanations as opposed to getting clarification on pressing issues. Cut all of that humble language out of your jargon and just express whatever you might be thinking - and do it with certainty," says Zaucha.

6. Be Mindful Of Your Body Language

In all honesty, you can feel 100% good assuming you become more mindful of how you decide to introduce yourself. "Whether it's your non-verbal communication or what you are wearing, ensure you look certain. Sit and stand tall. Wear a business-fitting dress. Visually engage. Grin without hesitation and have a confident handshake. These activities all appear to be basic, however actual impressions are a higher priority than you might understand," says Zaucha.

7. Practice It Every Day

"Working on being certain is an incredible beginning stage. The more you make it happen, the better you will get at it," says Zaucha. The more you work on being fearless, the better you can turn into. Ensure you converse with yourself all the more decidedly and encircle yourself with things that will satisfy you.

8. Observe Your Successes

"Certainty will transform your considerations right into it, and that activity will assist you with accomplishing anything you put your energy into. Also, remember to observe — and celebrate — your triumphs when they occur," says Zaucha. Regardless of how little your triumphs are, you ought to celebrate them. This act can support your soul and permit you to recall the amount of a boss you are.

9. Sort Out What Your Learning Style Is

It very well may be not difficult to feel crushed when you feel like you're unique from another person. You probably won't feel adequate because somebody advances speedier than you, however, everybody advances contrastingly and you shouldn't lose certainty thus. All things considered, attempt to sort out your learning style so you can defeat your trepidation and gain certainty. "Experience and authenticity are vital. At the point when you are mastering another expertise: realize your learning style (for instance: do you want to plunge your toe in the shallow end, or do you make a plunge?) Research all you can to figure out what it truly takes to significantly improve at something you need to, and make a sensible arrangement," says NY state-authorized marriage and family specialist Gracie Landes in a meeting with Bustle over email.

10. Make sure To Love Yourself For Who You Are

At times you don't feel sufficient because you contrast yourself with others. Stop this. You want to recall that you bring such a huge amount to the table and the world would be so unique without you. Love yourself for what your identity is. You should be praised for being you. "At the point when I have these sentiments and contemplations that I am simply not adequate at work, in that frame of mind, in my family, and so on, I attempt to continuously remind myself to cherish myself for who I truly am. I generally attempt to name something like three things that I love about myself and that I'm pleased with being great at. I comprehend that it's unimaginable for an individual to be everything to everybody and to be wonderful at everything," says CEO and prime supporter of Grabr Daria Rebenok in a meeting with Bustle over email.

11. Quit Overthinking It

If you're in any way similar to me, you struggle not overthinking everything. In any case, this perspective is poisonous and can hurt your self-assurance. "Not feeling 'sufficient' is a side effect of reasoning of oneself to an extreme. We want to escape our memorable selves which lie unlike the surface for us. The power that we have lays torpid under all the relentless reasoning," says contemplation master and Topdeck MOVE representative Biet Simkin in a meeting with Bustle over email.

12. Work On Your Well-being

Truly, you won't have an extraordinary outlook on yourself if you don't feel far better from the inside. You want to find an opportunity to keep up with your well-being to help your certainty and move past your apprehension about not being sufficient. "One of the primary things we believe that should do with the energy we save changes it in our contemplations. I don't completely accept that we want to surrender life to contemplate or surrender want to reflect. A remarkable opposite, I have faith in progress, world travel, extravagance, fun, sex, and so forth.! This is one reason I banded together with Topdeck Travel for the send-off of their MOVE program. With Topdeck's health program, we can give individuals an encounter that is profound while they travel and [push] their cutoff points and psyches when out and about is the best juxtaposition for contemplation that there is. In this day and age we don't have to surrender our possessions to arrive at illumination," says Simkin.

13. Advise Yourself That You're Not The Only One Who Feels Like This

Recollect a certain something: everybody has felt such at some point in their life. It's generally expected. Be that as it may, you would rather not need to manage this apprehension about not being sufficient until the end of your life. Assume responsibility by sorting out how you can fight this idea and become more certain. "I generally attempt to be consistent with myself, as I'm attempting to comprehend the wellspring of my self-uncertainty and how I can function around it and further develop it. I continually encircle myself with individuals who value me and back me and see a superior viewpoint in me, that occasionally I don't find in myself. Understanding that you're not by any means the only one that feels as such is significant.

Indeed, even individuals who appear to be that they have everything feel like they are not adequate in that frame of mind their life.

Even though it's normal to feel like you're not sufficient occasionally, you need to conquer your apprehension about not being adequate by not overthinking things, commending your victories, and chipping away at your prosperity.

www.ingramcontent.com/pod-product-compliance
Lightning Source LLC
LaVergne TN
LVHW050346160826
845677LV00014B/3818

9798351619361